Editor
Carmen Andrew, Ph.D.

Editorial Project Manager
Ina Massler Levin, M.A.

Editor-in-Chief
Sharon Coan, M.S. Ed.

Cover Artist
Cheri Macoubrie Wilson

Art Coordinator
Cheri Macoubrie Wilson

Creative Director
Elayne Roberts

Imaging
Ralph Olmedo, Jr.

Product Manager
Phil Garcia

Publisher
Mary D. Smith, M.S. Ed.

How to Write a Research Report

Grades 6–8

Author

Mari Lu Robbins, M.A.

Teacher Created Resources, Inc.
6421 Industry Way
Westminster, CA 92683
www.teachercreated.com

ISBN: 978-1-57690-492-3

©1999 Teacher Created Resources, Inc.
Reprinted, 2009
Made in U.S.A.

Table of Contents

Introduction 3

Getting Started

   Getting Started 4

   Selecting a Topic 5

   Brainstorming 6

   Types of Reports 7

   Getting Started Checklist 8

Finding and Organizing Information

   Finding Information 9

   The Dewey Decimal System 10

   Practice Using the Dewey Decimal System 11

   Card Catalog 12

   Library of Congress System 13

   Evaluating Information 14

   How to Think Critically 15

   Quiz on Critical Thinking 16

   Finding Information on the Internet 17

   Online Research Quiz 18

   Using Internet Resources 19

   Tips for Using a Search Engine 20

   Search Engines 21

   Searching Subject Directories 22

   Checklist for Evaluating Internet Sources 24

   Using CD-ROMs 25

   Hints for Taking Good Notes 26

   Setting Up a Bibliography Card Collection 27

Prewriting

   Thesis Statement 28

   Steps to Writing a Thesis Statement 29

   Making a Topic Outline 30

   Topic Outline 31

   Making a Sentence Outline 32

Writing

   Summarizing, Paraphrasing, and Quoting 33

   Taking the Plagiarism Pledge 34

   The Form of a Research Report 35

   Paragraph Transitions 36

   Word Bridges 37

   Revising Your Research Report 38

   Citing Resources 39–40

   Using Footnotes and Endnotes 41

   Using Parenthetical Citations 42

   Model Report 43–45

Glossary of Research Terms 46

Resources 47

Answer Key 48

Introduction

Writing a research report does not have to be a difficult task that your students will try to avoid. Once your students learn a systematic approach to writing research papers, they may find they actually enjoy the writing process more, and you will dread reading their papers less. By researching and writing about a topic, your students will learn more new information and gain more understanding than with almost any other learning experience. *How to Write a Research Report* will help you teach your students how to take the pain out of writing a research report by turning the process into a series of easy steps. The result will be well thought-out, clearly written papers of which you and they will be proud.

This book is divided into the following sections:

Getting Started

Students will learn what a research report is and how to translate the writing assignment into a completed work. They will learn the importance of understanding exactly what is being asked of them. They will learn about different types of reports and how to decide what type they are to write. Students will learn how to brainstorm possible topics for their papers, how to narrow down the possibilities, and how to focus on a manageable topic.

Finding and Organizing Information

Students will learn sources of information for their research topics. They will be introduced to two systems for locating books in the library, plus search engines to find information on the Internet. Students will learn how to differentiate between fact and opinion, how to think critically, and how to evaluate what they read. They will learn how to save a large collection of facts and figures and organize them into manageable and recognizable clusters of data and ideas.

Prewriting

Students will learn how to use the data they have collected to form the basis for their writing. They will learn to focus the data into thesis statements and topic outlines. They will learn to transform topic outlines into sentence outlines from which they will be able to write their research reports. The students will become familiar with the standard, five-paragraph form for written reports.

Writing

Students will learn to expand their outlines into fully developed research reports by writing first drafts, revising, and writing final drafts. They will learn to incorporate their thesis statements into the introductions and conclusions of their papers and how to cite resources in a way that will be acceptable throughout their educational careers.

Getting Started

The Importance of Being Early

A research report is a paper written using information obtained from a variety of sources. Locating the information and writing the report takes time. It is easy to put off until tomorrow what you need to get done today. However, when it comes to writing an assigned research report, you need to get started early. If you wait until just before the assignment is due, you will find yourself with the impossible task of trying to do research and writing a paper in a very short amount of time. You will end up with a poor paper and a poor grade.

Students who write the best papers and get the best grades are usually the ones who get started early. You want to write a good paper, and you want to get a good grade. Do the responsible thing. Start thinking about your paper as soon as you get the assignment. Let your mind generate ideas. Then, the first chance you get, sit down and start planning your paper. If you divide the task into a series of steps, you will find that writing the paper is easier and more manageable. You might even enjoy it!

Understanding the Assignment

Sometimes students do not really understand what is expected of them. One teacher may be very explicit in stating exactly how students are to do the report. Another teacher may give more general instructions, leaving the main responsibility of selecting a topic and deciding how to write the report to the student.

Obviously, it is easier to write a paper when you know ahead of time precisely what is expected. That is not always going to happen. A basic rule for any writing assignment is to write for your reader. In this case, your reader will be your teacher. If your teacher has not given you precise instructions, it is your responsibility to ask for clearer directions. You need to know the following:

- What kind of research report does the teacher expect?

- What kind of research does the teacher want you to do?

- On what will your grade be based?

You need the answers to these questions before you can get started on the assignment. Once you have this information, you are ready to begin the process of selecting a topic, setting deadlines for each step, searching for information, organizing your information, and writing your report. Keep these two adages in mind when beginning your research report:

> You probably will not know the answers until you ask the questions.

> If you don't know where you're going, you won't know when you get there.

Selecting a Topic

The next step in writing a research paper is selecting a topic. Begin with a general topic. Even if your teacher has assigned your topic, it is probably general. You will want a topic that is not too broad and not too narrow. The topic you choose should be interesting to you and to your reader. It must also meet the subject, length, and other criteria your teacher requires of you.

Topic that is too broad: The Space Race in the Twentieth Century

Topic that is not too broad: The *Apollo 11* Space Mission

Topic that is too narrow: Corvette Mag Wheels

Topic that is not too narrow: The Two Best-Rated Sports Cars of the Year

Select several general topics. Think of topics you are interested in or already know something about. Next, ask your classmates, your parents, and your teacher to give their ideas and reactions about how one of these subjects would work as a topic for a research paper. Page 6 describes three ways to brainstorm topics.

Possible topics are _____

_____

_____

When you have chosen the topic you like best, check it against this list. Revise your topic, if necessary.

Topic Checklist Criteria

☐ Is my topic too broad?

☐ Is my topic too narrow?

☐ Will my topic be interesting to readers?

☐ Is my topic interesting to me?

☐ Is my topic okay with my teacher?

The topic for my research paper is_____

_____

_____

Brainstorming

Brainstorming is a way to generate topics for a research paper. There are several ways to brainstorm, and the process can be done successfully either alone or in a group. Consider using one of these methods to help generate a suitable topic for your research paper.

Group Brainstorming

In this method of brainstorming, one member of the group acts as recorder, while each member says aloud any idea that comes to mind. As each person contributes an idea, the recorder writes the idea down without comment or discussion. After an agreed-upon length of time, the members of the group consider and discuss each of the options, finally narrowing the options down to a few upon which the members vote.

Lists

Lists are particularly useful when planning a comparison/contrast research paper. To make a list, columns are set up with headings, such as "alike" and "different." Everything a person can think of in which two or more things are alike is listed under "alike," and everything a person can think of in which they are different is listed under "different." Then one can compare and contrast using the entries in each list.

Clustering

Clustering is a way to narrow a general topic to a manageable size. For example, a student might want to write about France, but that topic is much too general for a 600- or 1,000-word report. The student can cluster possible subtopics around the general topic "France." After writing the general topic in the middle of the paper, write related subtopics around it. Then identify even more specific topics that relate to each subtopic. This picture will help you determine which topic has more appeal and, thus, help narrow down the possible areas for research.

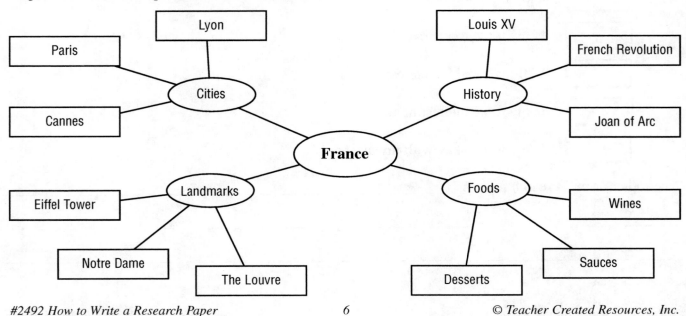

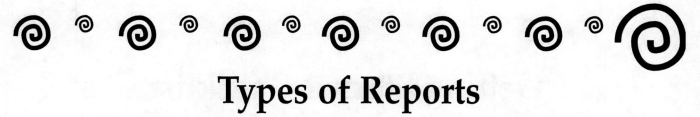

Types of Reports

There are many types of research reports, but all involve the same three steps: doing research, organizing information, and writing the report. Most research reports written for school will be descriptive, narrative, comparison/contrast, or cause and effect.

A descriptive report breaks a topic down into its parts so the reader can understand it. A narrative report tells a story of what has been discovered in the research. A comparison/contrast report demonstrates how two or more ideas or events are alike and different, or how they are and are not related. A cause and effect report seeks to prove that thing A is the cause of thing B. You will know what type of report to write by looking for keywords in the directions for the research report which your teacher gives you.

Keywords and What They Mean

1. Analyze

To *analyze* something, you break it into parts to find how the parts are related to each other. This helps you understand why events happened as they did or why you believe the way you do. When you analyze, you discuss cause and effect, explain your opinions or interpretations, and reveal facts and truths.

These key words are similar to analyze: *evaluate, examine, explain, describe.*

2. Argue or Support

To *argue* or *support* means to take a stand for or against an issue. You must give evidence and reasons why you feel the way you do.

These keywords are similar to argue or support: *justify, defend, persuade.*

3. Describe

To *describe* means to use carefully selected details to re-create an issue or idea so your reader can understand it. You may need to tell a story about what happened.

These key words are similar to describe: *narrate, relate, tell about, depict, portray.*

4. Discuss

To *discuss,* you tell about a subject from more than one perspective. You may point out several different aspects of the subject, or you may talk about several different points.

These keywords are similar to discuss: *compare, contrast.*

The keyword in my assignment is _____

Getting Started Checklist

Here is a checklist to guide you as you get started on your research report. Check each item as you complete it.

☐ I remembered the importance of starting early and began thinking about my research report as soon as it was assigned.

☐ I understand exactly what I am expected to do to complete this research report.

☐ I thought about general topics I might consider. I have decided on one of these general

topics: _____.

☐ I narrowed my topic down to_____.

☐ My topic will be interesting to the reader.

☐ My teacher has approved my topic.

☐ I have begun my preliminary research by reading the following:

_____

_____

_____

☐ My keyword is _____, which means that I will write a_____report.

☐ I have written my thesis statement. (Study pages 28 and 29 to learn how to write a thesis statement.) My thesis statement is . . .

_____

_____

☐ My next step will be _____.

Finding Information

Most of your research will be done in the library, so you need to know how a library is organized. The published materials you may wish to consult will include books and encyclopedias. In the library, you can also find information in firsthand materials such as letters, documents, novels, and news stories from newspapers and magazines. In order to locate this information, however, you will need to be familiar with *The Reader's Guide to Periodical Literature*, the Dewey Decimal System, and the Library of Congress System.

Because some of your research may be done on the computer, you need to know how to research online. Online library catalogs list all the items in a particular library, such as books, videos, maps, audio tapes, CDs, and periodicals. You will need to know how to use search engines and keywords. Each type of information you gather will need to be put into your bibliography according to the type of resource it is.

The types of information you look for will depend on where you are looking. If you are able to use the library of a high school or college, you will find certain types of materials. If you use the public library, you will find other materials. Go to the library you intend to use and see what resources it has. Answer these questions about the library you will use for your research.

Is the library computerized or does it have a card catalog? _____

Which classification system does it use? _____

Is there a reference librarian available? _____

      If so, what sorts of resources does she/he have? _____

_____

_____

Can you search in your library by subject? _____

Can you search in your library by author's name? _____

Can you search in your library by book title? _____

Can you search in your library by keyword? _____

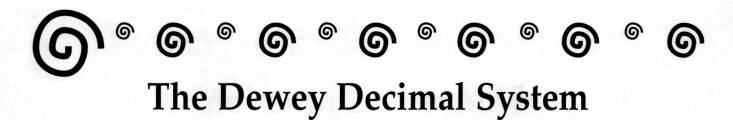

The Dewey Decimal System

The purpose of a classification system is to organize the way books and other materials are placed on the shelves in the library. Most libraries in the United States use the Dewey Decimal System, which was developed by Melvil Dewey. The Dewey Decimal System contains 10 general divisions numbered from 000 to 999.9. The general divisions are as follows:

000 to 099.9 Generalities
100 to 199.9 Philosophy and psychology
200 to 299.9 Religion
300 to 399.9 Social sciences
400 to 499.9 Language
500 to 599.9 Natural sciences and mathematics
600 to 699.9 Technology (Applied sciences)
700 to 799.9 The Arts
800 to 899.9 Literature and rhetoric
900 to 999.9 Geography and history

Within each of these general divisions, the system is further divided into more specific categories. For example, the general division for social sciences (300 to 399.9) is divided into the following smaller divisions:

300 to 309.9 Sociology and anthropology
310 to 319.9 General statistics
320 to 329.9 Political science
330 to 339.9 Economics
340 to 349.9 Law
350 to 359.9 Public administration
360 to 369.9 Social services, associations
370 to 379.9 Education
380 to 389.9 Commerce, communications, transport
390 to 399.9 Customs, etiquette, folklore

With the Dewey Decimal System of organization, each nonfiction book in the library can be assigned a number. Books are placed on the shelves in the library in numerical order. Once you know the number of the subject you wish to research, you can go directly to that section of the library shelves to find what is available in your subject. To find the number of the subject you wish to research, look in the card catalog or library computer.

Go to the library and find the Dewey Decimal System number for books on the subjects on the following page.

Practice Using the Dewey Decimal System

In your library, use the following subject titles to find the correct Dewey Decimal number of each.

1. _____ Classical Greek Literature

2. _____ Folktales of Ireland

3. _____ History of the Roman Catholic Church

4. _____ German grammar

5. _____ History of Ancient Sumeria

6. _____ Electrical engineering

7. _____ Drama and performing arts

8. _____ Journalism and publishing

9. _____ The philosophy of Ancient China

10. _____ The periodic table of chemical elements

11. _____ History of the early Christian Church

12. _____ Cultural anthropology

13. _____ Explorers to South America

14. _____ World art museums

15. _____ English literature

16. _____ The geography of France

17. _____ Linguistics

18. _____ Printmaking

19. _____ Manuscripts and rare books

20. _____ Life sciences

Card Catalog

The card catalog uses the Dewey Decimal System. In the card catalog, books are listed three ways: by subject, by title, and by author. The cards are arranged in alphabetical order. In a card catalog, each book would be listed three times, as shown here.

Subject Card

Subject
J629.132 Dor
Aeronautics—Accident Investigation
Dorman, Michael F.
Detectives of the Sky; Investigating Aviation Accidents. Watts. ©1976.
Index. Bibliography

Title Card

Title
J629.132 Dor
Detectives of the Sky
Dorman, Michael F.
Detectives of the Sky: Investigating Aviation Accidents. Watts. ©1976.

Author Card

Author
Dorman, Michael F.
J629.132 Dor
Includes index. Describes the work of government investigators of airplane crashes, citing types of accidents and specific crashes.
Bibliography: page 97
Subject Heading
1. Aeronautics—Accident Investigation

Reader's Guide To Periodical Literature

The *Reader's Guide to Periodical Literature* is an invaluable resource for locating magazine articles on a particular topic. Look up your research topic in the *Guide*. Once you identify those articles you would like to examine, note the title, date, and volume number of the magazines. In many libraries, the librarian will be able to help you locate the magazines, as only current editions are on the shelves.

Library of Congress System

The Library of Congress System for classifying books uses divisions by letters rather than numbers. Many college and university libraries use this system. These are the letters and titles of the main classes and a sampling of the subclasses used in the Library of Congress Classification System.

A - General Works AE—Encyclopedias AI—Indexes AN—Newspapers AP—Periodicals	**B - Philosophy** BH—Esthetics BJ—Ethics BL-BX—Religions, Mythology	**C - History** CC—Archaeology CT—Biography	**D - History** DA—Great Britain DC—France DD—Germany
E-F American and U.S. History	**G - Geography, Anthropology, and Folklore**	**H - Social Sciences** HA-HJ—Geography, Travel, Atlases	**J - Political Sciences** JF—Constitutional history JK—U.S. Constitutional history
K - Law	**L - Education**	**M - Music** ML—Literature of Music MT—Musical Instruction	**N - Fine Arts** NA—Architecture NB—Sculpture ND—Painting
P - Language and Literature PJ-PL—Oriental Languages PQ—Romance languages PS—American Literature PT—German Literature	**Q - Science** QA—Mathematics QB—Astronomy QD—Chemistry QL—Zoology QM—Human Anatomy	**R - Medicine** RA—Public Health RC—Internal Medicine, Sports Medicine RT—Nursing	**S - Agriculture** SD—Forestry SF—Veterinary Medicine
T - Technology and Engineering TA-TP—Engineering TR—Photography TT—Arts and Crafts	**U - Military Science**	**V - Naval Science**	**Z - Bibliography & Library Science**

Evaluating Information

When doing research, it is important that you learn to think critically about the information you find. Critical evaluation of information will help your whole life, not just when you are doing research. If you think carefully and analyze the materials you read, you will know whether you are receiving accurate information. Never assume that whatever you read in print is true and accurate just because it has been published. Many books and articles are printed that are completely inaccurate. Some slant the truth in a way that causes the unwary reader to believe what is not true. Remember, just as you want to write for your reader, other writers are writing what they want you as a reader to believe. Read carefully. What are some things you need to watch for?

Knowing the Difference Between Fact and Opinion

A **fact** is something that exists. It is truth; it is reality. An **opinion** is a judgment. It may be true, or it may not be.

> **Fact:** People must have air to breathe in order to live.
> **Opinion:** Perfume makes the air smell fresh.

Which of these statements state fact, and which are opinion? Why?

_____ 1. Dogs make good pets.

_____ 2. The United States is made up of 50 individual states.

_____ 3. People need to learn at least one language besides their own.

_____ 4. Most universities require entering students to have taken mathematics.

_____ 5. Good students should study two hours every night.

_____ 6. Green vegetables contain many vitamins needed for health.

_____ 7. Milk is good for everyone.

_____ 8. Good parents always give their children everything they need.

_____ 9. *Forrest Gump* is a good movie.

_____ 10. *Forrest Gump* stars Tom Hanks.

_____ 11. *Time* magazine is one of the best magazines.

_____ 12. Different writers with varying ideas write for *Time* magazine.

_____ 13. Some magazines are published just to make money.

_____ 14. An almanac contains interesting facts.

Write one fact and one opinion about a book you've read recently.

Fact _____

Opinion _____

How to Think Critically

When you think critically, you question what you read, hear, and think about things. You do not just accept what someone says just because she/he says it. Does the person who says something which sounds true have the background and knowledge to know what she/he is talking about? You need to question yourself and your own decisions to be sure you are making the best decisions under the circumstances. Write **yes** or **no** next to each question.

When choosing research materials to use in your research report, ask yourself these questions about each source.

Name of source_____

1. Does this source help answer the questions I need to answer? _____

2. Is this source biased; does it try to make me take one side or another? _____

3. Does this source make broad generalizations, such as boys don't show their feelings or girls cry too much? _____

4. Does this source give easy answers and make complex things sound too simple? _____

5. Does this source consider more than one side of a question? _____

6. What background does the writer of this source have that makes him/her an expert about the subject? _____

When writing your research report, ask yourself these questions about what you are writing.

1. Am I generalizing too much? _____

2. Am I oversimplifying? _____

3. Have I considered differing opinions? _____

4. Have I withheld my judgment until after reading all my sources? _____

5. Have I read each source carefully? _____

6. Is this source appropriate for school use? _____

Quiz on Critical Thinking

Answer the following questions about how to evaluate research data.

1. You are writing a paper about drug abuse. Which of these is the most reliable source of information about this subject?

   A _____ Your neighbor who has been in a drug abuse program
   B _____ Dr. Dean Edell
   C _____ *The Physician's Desk Reference of Drugs and Alcohol Abuse*

2. You are writing a paper about the Persian Gulf War of 1990. Which of these is the best source of unbiased information?

   A _____ An article in *MAD* magazine
   B _____ An article in *Newsweek* magazine
   C _____ A political commercial on television

3. You are writing a research paper. Which of these is the narrowest topic for you to write about?

   A _____ Communications systems in the 20th century
   B _____ The life of Alexander Graham Bell
   C _____ Bell's invention of the telephone

4. You are writing a paper about the use of technology in school. Who is the best source of information on this subject?

   A _____ The technology teacher in your school
   B _____ The owner of a local computer store
   C _____ The president of a software company

5. You are considering becoming a doctor and are writing a paper about medicine. Which of these is the best source of information for you to use?

   A _____ Your family doctor
   B _____ A five-year-old copy of a medical journal which your uncle gave you
   C _____ The latest issue of the *American Medical Association Journal*

6. You are writing a paper on contagious diseases in public school. Which of these is your best source of information?

   A _____ Your school health aide
   B _____ Your teacher
   C _____ The last six issues of *The Bulletin of the Center for Disease Control*

After choosing your answers thoughtfully, discuss them with your teacher and the class.

Finding Information on the Internet

Picture millions of computers all hooked together by a common thread, somewhat like a giant spider web, stretched in many directions and operated by millions of people at the same time. On this giant web, people can send and receive electronic mail (e-mail), join groups of people with the same interests as their own, talk about things which concern them, search for information on many different topics, and download text, graphics, sound, and software. This is the Internet.

Before the early 1990s, the information that was available on the Internet had been placed there solely by educators, scientists, students, and the government. Now, however, the widespread use of the Internet by ordinary people has grown to the point where just about anyone who has a computer and a modem can put anything online. Some material put online is personal, some professional, and some is educational.

Much of the information you will find online is not what you want to use for a school research report. While there is a wealth of good information on the Internet, there is also a great amount that is not good. You must use your best judgment when looking for information. Look for educational sites, scientific sites, and professionally constructed sites. *If a piece of information is not appropriate for school use, do not use it.*

What you can find online:

- a limited number of free encyclopedias and dictionaries
- encyclopedia and dictionary resources which have a fee or subscription charge
- information posted by educators as part of their teaching
- personal homepages posted by students and others
- excerpts from current and recent issues of magazines and newspapers
- a limited number of electronic magazines and journals
- information provided by government agencies, such as the Library of Congress and NASA
- information provided by nonprofit organizations on their areas of interest
- complete text of works (books, plays, and stories) whose copyrights have expired
- a limited number of single-volume reference works

What you cannot find online:

- most reference works such as encyclopedias, at least not for free
- books, plays, and short stories still under copyright
- full text nonfiction books on scholarly subjects
- most scholarly journal articles
- newspaper and magazine articles published prior to 1994
- many of the reference books, such as author information volumes, which are available from your library's reference librarian

Online Research Quiz

Complete the following quiz by writing **Yes** in front of sites you could use as a source for a research report and **No** for those you should not. Discuss your answers with your class and your teacher.

_____ 1. The English Department of Purdue University for a report on grammar.

_____ 2. NASA for a report on the *Challenger* mission.

_____ 3. An article about AIDS from a medical journal published in 1985.

_____ 4. *Encyclopedia Americana* for information on World War I.

_____ 5. Scientific article from the current issue of *USA Today* or the *New York Times*.

_____ 6. The full text of *Hamlet* or *Romeo and Juliet* by Shakespeare.

_____ 7. The homepage of Pleasant Valley High School in Chico, California.

_____ 8. A 1995 article from the *Journal of Anthropology* for a report on culture.

_____ 9. Articles on journalism from the *Encyclopedia Britannica* for a report on communications.

_____ 10. The script of your favorite movie for a report on the American Revolution.

_____ 11. The text of the year's Newbery Award-winning novel for a report on literary awards.

_____ 12. The homepage of your favorite computer teacher for a report on biology.

_____ 13. An article in last week's *Time* magazine for a report on medicine.

_____ 14. The short stories of Edgar Allen Poe for a report on the short story.

_____ 15. The poetry of Emily Dickinson for a report on psychology.

_____ 16. Information from the newspaper about last week's shuttle flight to Mars.

_____ 17. Articles on polar bears from *Encyclopedia Britannica*.

_____ 18. A history textbook about the American Revolution.

Using Internet Resources

Using the Internet is not quite as easy as visiting your library. The Internet does not have a research librarian, nor is there a regular system of cataloging such as the Dewey Decimal System or the Library of Congress Catalog. To use the Internet, you will need to know how to find your way around on it. Searching the Internet for information will become easier as more people go online. For now, however, the resources available include the following:

- search engines
- meta-search engines
- Usenet newspaper guides
- e-mail address guides

- guides to library collections and resources
- book guides
- guides to periodicals
- subject directories

Using A Search Engine

Most of the information you find on the Internet, you will find using a search engine. There are, however, many search engines; they do not all search in the same way, nor do they all search the same files. Therefore, you need to become familiar with various search engines. What you do not find on one, you might find on another. However, searching through the files of first one, then another, can be time-consuming. You can not expect that you will always save time by using the Internet rather than going to the library. Using the Internet does offer the advantage of being able to work in your own home, if you have a computer and modem and belong to an Internet Provider Service.

A search engine will provide you with a list of hypertext files, which are underlined and highlighted. When you click on a highlighted hypertext file name, new files will appear on your computer screen. Since most search engines are commercial, you will be shown many files that advertise. Information from these will not be appropriate for use in your research paper. You will need to learn how to scroll through the files to eliminate those that are simply commercial. Most search engines are free, however, and educational sites are generally included alongside commercial ones. Knowing Internet address domains will help you select appropriate educational sites. Internet address domains are as follows:

com—commercial and business
edu—educational institutions
gov—government agencies
mil—military organizations
net—network resources
org—other organizations

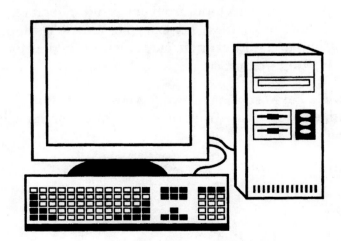

Tips for Using a Search Engine

1. To use a search engine, you need to identify a **keyword** for the engine to search. Keywords are words that represent the concepts of your topic. If you enter the keyword "Lincoln," you will get thousands of documents about Lincoln. Entries will include Abraham Lincoln, as well as the towns and schools named Lincoln. To narrow your search, enter "Abraham Lincoln."

2. Use keywords that would be most likely to get best results. Be specific. For example, to learn about the welfare system in California, use "welfare AND California."

3. If you enter AND between two words, you will get files containing both words.

4. If you enter OR between two words, you will get files containing at least one of the words.

5. If you use NOT before a word, no files containing that word will appear.

6. ALL will act the same as AND.

7. ANY will act the same as OR.

8. Using an asterisk (*) after a word will bring up files with all the many variations of a word. For example, "human*" will bring up "humanist," "humane," and "humanistic."

9. When you first open the homepage of the search engine, first go to **Help**, **FAQ** (Frequently Asked Questions) to learn how to best use the search engine. Print this page for reference.

10. Compare different search engines to see how they work differently.

11. Print out the first page of each search both for finding it again and for citation.

12. Place your favorite sites in the Bookmarks or Favorite Places file in your computer.

13. Meta-Search Engines check several search engines and show their files.

14. Use subject directories from universities, libraries, and search engines as you would subject catalogs in libraries. For example, Yahoo! has directories for **Arts and Humanities**, **Business**, **Computers**, **Education**, etc. A university directory might list **English**, **History**, **Philosophy**, **Writing Center**, etc.

Choose a keyword that relates to your research project. On the back of this paper, list the first 10 documents you locate from three separate search engines. Underline the ones that are educational sites.

Search Engines

The following are search engines you may find useful while doing research for your paper.

Alta Vista—http://altavista.digital.com

Infoseek—http://www.infoseek.com

Lycos—http://www.lycos.com

Galaxy—http://www.einet.net

Yahoo!—http://www.yahoo.com

Excite—http://www.excite.com

GeoCities—http://www.geocities.com

Hotbot—http://www.hotbot.com

Magellan—http://magellan.excite.com

Webcrawler—http://www.webcrawler.com

Northern Light—http://www.nlsearch.com

Meta-Search Engines

Meta-Search Engines check several search engines for information on your topic. The following are popular Meta-Search Engines:

Dogpile—http://www.dogpile.com

Inference Find—http://infind.com

MetaCrawler—http://www.metacrawler.com

Choose three of the above search engines. Go to each. Answer the following for each.

1. Name of engine_____

2. Does this engine have a directory?_____

   If so, on the back of this page list the entries in the directory.

3. Is this a commercial site? How can you tell? _____

Searching Subject Directories

Many universities, libraries, and other organizations have online subject directories. These are similar to the subject catalogs in libraries and can be useful to the student doing research. Most search engines also have subject directories. The quality of these directories varies. Some directories are regularly evaluated by experts, and others are not so carefully watched. Therefore, you need to do some looking and evaluating of your own to determine whether or not a directory is worth using.

A good directory can be valuable in giving you an overview of the topic that interests you. Some will lead you to homepages. These may provide you with more information than you thought available, such as magazines, organizations, and books. Most are arranged so you can go from a general topic to a more specific one. Try out each directory and print out and bookmark the ones that are valuable to you.

Popular Subject Directories

Search engines—http://[search engine name].com

WWW Virtual Library—http://vlib.org

INFOMINEScholarly Internet Resource Collections—http://lib-www.ucr.edu

Librarians' Index to the Internet—http://sunsite.berkeley.edu/InternetIndex

UCB Library and Internet Resources by Subject—http://lib.berkeley.edu

Britannica Internet Guide—http://www.ebig.com

BUBL Link—http://www.bubl.ac.uk

Magellan—http://www.mckinley.com

Check out at least three of these subject directories. Which is most valuable to you for finding information on the following subjects?

1. hotels in New York City _____

   _____

2. homeschooling, grades 7–12 _____

   _____

3. current medical science _____

   _____

4. cultures of the world _____

   _____

Searching Subject Directories *(cont.)*

5. publications on computing _____

6. how to buy a new automobile _____

7. shopping online _____

8. jobs in England _____

Search Guides to Periodicals

You can use online periodical guides to find magazines and periodicals related to your subject just as you use the *Reader's Guide to Periodical Literature* in the library. Online you will find indexes to the publications and may access entire articles.

Many magazines and periodicals have their own pages. To see whether the one you want does, try these:

http://www.[title of magazine or journal].com

or

Go to a search engine, type in the name of the magazine you want, and click search,

or

type the subject AND journals or periodicals in search box and click search.

Periodical Guides

These are the most easily accessible online guides to periodicals.

Ecola Newsstand—-http://www.ecola.com

Internet Public Library Reading Room Newspapers—-
http://www.ipl.org/reading/news

Internet Public Library Reading Room Serials—-
http://www.ipl.org/reading/serials

Use these periodical guides to find magazines or journals on these subjects. Which is best?

1. linguistics _____

2. newspapers in North Dakota _____

3. travel in Europe _____

4. science magazines _____

Checklist for Evaluating Internet Sources

Ask yourself these questions about each Internet source you find. You should be able to answer yes to all or most of these.

_____ **Is this site an edu, org, gov, or mil site?** These are the sites which are generally the most reliable ones. Commercial (com) sites contain advertising and articles which may be slanted one way or another.

_____ **Is the author a well-known expert, perhaps connected with an established institution?** Remember, anyone can put anything on the Internet, so you do not want to believe something just because it is online any more than you want to believe something just because it is in print.

_____ **Is the publisher a university, professional organization, government agency, or well-known publisher?** Avoid publishers that exist only on the Internet. There are so-called vanity publishers on the Internet whom people pay to publish their material. There are also organizations such as cults and other groups that establish Web sites just to promote their own philosophies.

_____ **Do the hyperlinks given take you to educational sites?**

_____ **Is a bibliography provided which shows high quality sources?**

_____ **Does the site provide quality sources that you can check out for yourself?**

_____ **Is there a recent publication date showing that the information is current?**

_____ **Is the information given based on facts rather than the opinions of the author?** Remember that anyone can put anything on the Internet without having to back up what he/she says with factual information. Beware of information that is clearly written to persuade you into believing what the author wants you to believe.

_____ **Is the information written for people who are seriously interested?** Beware of information you get from chat lines.

Using CD-ROMs

CD-ROMs are very useful for doing research in the classroom, computer center, or library. They are small and contain a great deal of information on one small, compact disk. The most useful include encyclopedias, dictionaries, atlases, history and science collections, and reference guides to magazines such as *Time* and *National Geographic*. For the most efficient use, CD-ROMs should be booted up before class and a system of sign-ups or scheduling established. The following are some that are commonly used in middle school classrooms and libraries:

American Heritage: The History of the United States for Young People. Byron Press Multimedia Co., The American National, Prentice-Hall, Upper Saddle River, NJ, 1996.

The Animals True Multimedia Experience. Macintosh, Novato, 1992–1993.

Catropedia: The Ultimate World Reference Atlas. Apple, DK.

Color Photos for Mac 5000 Megapack Photos. Nova Development Corporation, Calabasses, CA, 1996.

Compton's Interactive Atlas. The Learning Co., Cambridge, MA, 1998.

Discover the Joy of Science. Zane Publishing Co., Dallas, TX, 1998.

Encarta Encyclopedia Deluxe. Microsoft, USA.

Encyclopedia Britannica CD. Merriam-Webster Inc., 1994-1998.

Grolier Multimedia Encyclopedia. Grolier Interactive, Danbury, CT.

History of the World. DK Multimedia, Dorling Kindersley, NY, 1998.

Mindscape World Atlas & Almanac. Mindscape, Novato, CA, 1996.

Rand-McNally New Millennium World Atlas Deluxe, "Interactive." Rand McNally, Skokie, IL, 1998.

Scientific American Library The Universe, with Complete Planetarium, Planet-Building Simulation Game, Voyage from Atoms to Stars, and Tour of Solar System and Universe. Byron Press Multimedia, USA, 1998.

Time Reference Edition Almanac. Time Magazine, New York, 1994.

Webster's International Encyclopedia. Multimedia 2000, Seattle, WA, 1998.

Webster's New World Family Discovery Library II. McMillan, USA, 1998.

A World of Animals, 5 CD Nature Encyclopedia. Countertop, Redmond, WA, 1998.

World Book 1999 Family Reference Suite, containing Encyclopedia of Literature, Biographical Dictionary, Intermediate Dictionary, and Medical Desk Dictionary. World Book Inc., San Diego, CA.

Hints for Taking Good Notes

There is no magic way to take good notes. However, here are a few suggestions about how to take the best notes you can on the research you do.

- Get an understanding of the whole piece of material before you decide to use it.

- Skim over the material to make sure it is appropriate for what you want. Read section headings, look at photos, maps, and charts, and read the captions underneath.

- Make a bibliography card for each book, periodical, CD-ROM, and Internet service you use before you begin to take notes. Instructions for writing bibliography cards are on page 27.

- Write clearly and neatly so you will be able to read the notes when you are ready to use them.

- Keep a file box of index cards on which to write your notes. This will help you sort your notes when you are ready to start organizing your report.

- Put only one piece of information on a card.

- Write on only one side of a card.

- Paraphrase information you think you want to use.

- Put quotation marks around any direct quote and note the page number on which you found it.

- Note the name of the person who said anything you will want to quote indirectly.

- Write down all information even if you are unsure you will use it. You can always skip it later.

- Take complete notes of important information.

- Use key words to indicate the nature of the material.

- Be accurate. Be neat.

- Keep all of your notes until your paper is finished. You never know when you will need a piece of information.

Remember: Taking good notes is half of writing a good paper.

Setting up a Bibliography Card Collection

As you do the research for your paper, make one bibliography card for each source: books, periodicals, CD-ROMs, and Internet sources. The bibliography should be written on 3" x 5" index cards that you keep in a file box. A sample card is at the bottom of the page. Include the following information for each source:

Books

Author's name
Title of book, underlined
Name of editor or translator
Edition
Number of volume(s)
Publisher
Publication city
Publication date
Page number(s)
Library call number

CD-ROMs

Author's name
Title of material, in quotation marks
Date of material
Database title underlined
Publication medium (CD-ROM)
Vendor's name, if relevant
Electronic publication date

Periodicals

Author's name
Title of article, in quotation marks
Title of periodical, underlined
Series number
Volume number
Publication date
Page number(s)

Internet Services

Author's name
Title of article or document, in quotes
Title of journal or newsletter, if
    appropriate
Volume or issue number
Publication date, in parentheses
Number of pages, if given
Publication medium (online)
Computer network name
Access date

Sample Bibliography Cards for a Book

The bibliography is usually placed on a separate page at the end of the report. Entries are typically listed alphabetically by author's last name. See page 45 for an example.

Thesis Statement

Begin writing your research report by writing a thesis statement. The thesis statement is one sentence that will focus your paper. It will give your paper direction by saying in one full, declarative sentence what you want the entire paper to say. The statement will limit your topic to one narrow focus and point to the intended conclusion of your paper. This is the point you want your reader to get by reading your paper. The thesis statement comes in your introductory paragraph and will be restated in your concluding paragraph.

If you draw a diagram to illustrate just how your thesis statement fits into your report, you might draw it like this:

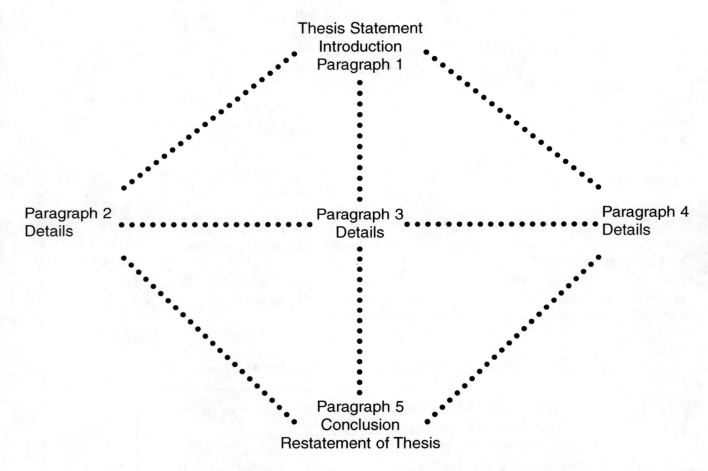

This diagram illustrates a standard, five-paragraph essay, but the same structure will fit a research report of almost any length. What you need to remember is that to be coherent and effective, your research report must have a clear beginning, middle, and end all focused around your thesis statement.

Write your definition of a thesis statement here. _____

_____

Steps to Writing a Thesis Statement

The purpose of writing a research report is to convince your reader of the point you want to make about a topic by backing it up with information which supports that point. In order for you to do this and for you to even know what it is you want to say, you must first get all your information together, then organize it clearly. You must answer certain questions about your topic and your information. Then you will be able to write the thesis statement for your report. Use this checklist.

☐ I have found an interesting general topic.

My general topic is _____.

It is interesting because _____.

☐ I have narrowed the topic down.

My final topic is _____.

It is significant because _____.

☐ I have written bibliography cards for all materials I used.

☐ I have taken notes without plagiarizing.

☐ I have put materials in order of importance.

☐ I have read over my notes, checked my bibliography cards, and thought about what I have learned from my research.

☐ Answer this question: What is the point I want my reader to get from my report?

_____

_____

NOW, and only now, are you ready to write your thesis statement.

☐ My thesis statement is _____

_____

Making a Topic Outline

Writing a topic outline is the next step in writing your research report. A well-constructed topic outline serves a dual purpose. It organizes what until now has been a hodgepodge of information, notes, and cards, and it makes the actual writing of the report relatively easy. All that is left to do when the topic outline is finished is to write a sentence outline, revise, and proofread your writing.

Hints for Outlining

1. **Make your topic outline first.** Classify ideas under topic headings that support your thesis statement.
2. **Have two or more divisions under each topic** with at least two subdivisions under each of those.
3. **Look at your topic outline** to see what information you still have not collected. Go back to the library to find what you have left out. If information is not available, change your outline.
4. **Use the sample form** on page 31 to set up your outline like this:

Thesis statement: Franklin Delano Roosevelt was a strong president in a time when the United States needed one.

I. Strong leadership needed

    A. Great Depression

        1. High unemployment

        2. Hungry people

        3. No job security or old age pensions

    B. Much unrest in the world

        1. Hitler and the rise of fascism

            a. First wanted to conquer Europe

            b. Then wanted to conquer the world

        2. Japan and the conquest of China

            a. Wanted to conquer China

            b. Wanted to control the Pacific

II. Roosevelt able to make firm, but difficult decisions

    A. Bank holiday

        1. Kept people from making run on banks

        2. Department of the Treasury examined every bank's books.

Keep your outline in a logical, reasonable order.

Topic Outline

Thesis statement:_____

_____

I. _____

  A._____

    1. _____

    2. _____

  B._____

    1. _____

    2. _____

      a. _____

      b. _____

II._____

  A._____

    1. _____

    2. _____

      a. _____

        (1.)_____

        (2.)_____

      b. _____

  B._____

III. _____

  A._____

    1. _____

    2. _____

  B._____

    1. _____

    2. _____

Conclusion _____

_____

Making a Sentence Outline

The topic outline you made earlier now needs to be changed into a sentence outline. Look at the following examples:

Topic Outline	Sentence Outline
I. Strong leadership needed	Franklin Roosevelt came to the presidency in a time when strong leadership was needed.
A. Great Depression	Most of the world was in the grip of the Great Depression.
1. high unemployment	At no other time in our nation's history have so many people been unemployed.
2. hungry people	Millions of people lined up at soup kitchens daily for the only food they'd get. With no money to buy food, people were starving.
3. no job security or old age pensions	People had no job security. There was little unemployment insurance, and the elderly did not have pensions.

Now write your own sentence outline. Change the topic outline you made on page 31 into a sentence outline. Begin your outline here and continue on your own paper. Summarize, paraphrase, or quote from your notes.

Thesis statement _____

_____

_____

I. _____

  A. _____

    1. _____

    2. _____

  B. _____

    1. _____

    2. _____

      a. _____

      b. _____

Summarizing, Paraphrasing, and Quoting

Summarizing, paraphrasing, and quoting are three ways of using the information you found in researching your report. When you summarize, paraphrase, and quote correctly, you will avoid the problem of plagiarism. These techniques take practice, however.

The following paragraph is reproduced from an interdisciplinary unit on Native Americans published by Teacher Created Resources, Inc. Assume you found this paragraph while doing your research and want to incorporate it into your research report.

> Long ago in Middle America, there were small, wandering groups of hunters who were equipped with flaked knives, pebble tools, and choppers. Half or more of their food they got from hunting, and the rest was from wild vegetable sources which included species that would later become domesticated plants such as gourds, pumpkins, peppers, and runner beans. Shortly after 6500 B.C., some inhabitants began to cultivate cotton, chili peppers, and a type of squash. The people became dependent on these plants, and as they did, they began to adjust their hunting patterns to seasonal changes. This encouraged two or three families to settle down together each year in order to cooperatively harvest these vegetable foods.

Practice summarizing, paraphrasing, and quoting by doing the following:

1. To **summarize**, read this passage and without looking at it again, rewrite the main points in your own words in three sentences or less. Do not include your own interpretations. Do not add your own ideas. After finishing, check your accuracy.

   _____

   _____

   _____

   _____

2. To **paraphrase**, read this passage and do not look at it again. Rewrite the passage in your own words including all the points made by the author. Do not offer your own ideas or interpretations. After finishing, check your accuracy.

   _____

   _____

   _____

   _____

3. To **quote**, copy the author's words exactly and place them within quotation marks. Include all punctuation and capitals. If there are errors in the passage, copy them exactly as they are. Immediately after the error write "(sic)," which is a Latin word meaning "so" or "thus." Use your own paper.

Taking the Plagiarism Pledge

Plagiarism is writing or using the words of someone else as though they were your own. It is dishonest and a violation of copyright law to use what someone else has written without giving the source credit. To acknowledge you will not use someone else's work as your own, take the following plagiarism pledge and sign it.

Plagiarism Pledge

Date _____

I, _____

do hereby promise that when writing a report I will do the following:

- When using or paraphrasing the words or material written by someone else in a report of my own, I will give that person credit by naming him or her.

- I will enclose exact material in quotation marks and name the author of the material.

- When paraphrasing the material of another, I will rewrite it in my own style and language.

- I will not simply rearrange the words of another person and claim them as my own.

- I will double-check the accuracy of any quotation I use and any citation I make.

- If I add or change words in a quotation, I will enclose them in brackets.

- I will not change the meaning of words written by another to a different meaning of my own.

- I will provide a bibliography of works I use showing the title of the work, the name of the author and publisher, and the publishing date, plus pages referred to.

Signed _____

The Form of a Research Report

Your research report will take a form similar to that of the five-paragraph essay. This is a standard form for most short, formally written papers. While many reports will follow this form exactly, some may have four paragraphs, or seven, or ten, or almost any number of total paragraphs depending on information available and length required. However, the same basic structure will be used, whatever the number of paragraphs. The first paragraph will be an introduction. The introduction will be followed by body paragraphs, and a conclusion will be at the end. No one part of the report is more important than any other part. Each part needs to work together with the others to make a clear, coherent paper which says what you want to say and convinces your reader of the points you want to make. Learn to follow this basic pattern of writing for any report you write in, or for, class. Knowing the form of the five-paragraph essay will help you with many of your school writing projects. The form of the five-paragraph report is illustrated on page 28.

The Introduction

The purpose of the first paragraph is to grab your reader's interest. You need to think carefully about how to write it. This paragraph will include your thesis statement, which controls and focuses the paper. The introduction states the point of your paper and lets your reader know you are going to tell him/her something new or different.

The Body Paragraphs

The paragraphs between the introduction and the conclusion give your reader details about the thesis you stated in your introductory paragraph. Each paragraph should begin with a topic sentence that ties this new paragraph to the preceding one. Each paragraph should follow the previous one in a logical order.

The Conclusion

The concluding paragraph is important. It ties your thesis statement together with all of your supporting details to bring your reader to the same conclusion that you have reached. The conclusion restates your thesis and shows how the thesis has been supported by the information presented in the body paragraphs.

Using the sentence outline you prepared, write a first draft of your report. Begin your introduction with Section I of your outline. Be certain to include your thesis statement in paragraph one. Use sections two to four of your outline to build the body paragraphs. Write each topic sentence based on Section I, II, or III of the sentence outline. Write a transition sentence at the end of each paragraph to lead into the following paragraph. Transition sentences are described on page 36. Write a strong conclusion. The conclusion should refer to your thesis and reiterate why the thesis is true. At the end of your report, include a bibliography of the resources you used.

Paragraph Transitions

Many students have difficulty writing the transitions necessary to get smoothly from one paragraph to another. It is helpful to think of transitions as bridges. Their purpose is to carry the reader from one place to another without falling off the main topic. There are four kinds of paragraph bridges: time bridges, series bridges, place bridges, and mechanical bridges. Fiction writers will sometimes use other kinds of bridges, such as flashbacks. However, for the purposes of writing a research report, you need to learn to use time bridges, place bridges, and series bridges.

Time Bridges

Time bridges serve to carry the reader from one time to another. The kinds of words you might use in a time bridge would be ones such as these:

> On a day in early summer . . .
>
> Four days later in another part of town . . .
>
> Exactly two months later . . .

Place Bridges

Place bridges serve to carry the reader from one place to another. The kinds of place bridges you might use would be ones such as these:

> That morning at the church . . .
>
> He threw the bicycle down by the fence and went . . .
>
> The Empire State Building came into view and . . .

Series Bridges

Series bridges give a feeling of time passing in small, incremental steps. The underlined phrases show the series of time marching on.

> Joan shivered <u>as she watched</u> her sister climb the hill. She still felt a stab of fear <u>two hours later</u> when Cicely hadn't come home. <u>As the afternoon wore on</u>, a little nagging continued in the back of her mind, and <u>by the time she finished</u> her homework, she knew she had to tell someone.

Use paragraph transitions in reports to signal that a new paragraph is about to begin.

Practice writing paragraph transitions on the back of this paper. Write three each of time bridges, place bridges and series bridges. When you finish, share what you have written with the class and your teacher. Discuss how these can help you move smoothly through your report.

Word Bridges

Word bridges help your writing flow smoothly from one part, idea, or thought to another. Word bridges are words or phrases that link one part of a sentence, one thought, or one part of a paragraph to another. They help connect parts and ideas so your reader will go from one to the other without having to question what is being said.

Words of Contrast

When **contrasting** two ideas or parts of a sentence or paragraph together, use one of these:

but	however	although
nevertheless	on the other hand	conversely

Words of Addition

When **adding** a sentence part or idea to another, use one of these:

furthermore	similarly	along with
moreover	for example	as well as

Words Showing Cause and Effect

When wishing to **show how one thing causes another**, use these:

as a result	therefore
consequently	because

Words Showing Time Change:

next	after	during
afterward	then	since
first	immediately	

Words Showing Location Change:

among	across	beside
between	behind	near
down	inside	

Words Pointing to a Summary:

consequently	finally
therefore	thus

Practice writing sentences using word bridges. On the back of this paper, write one sentence using a bridge showing contrast, one showing addition, one showing cause and effect, one showing time change, one showing location change, and one that points to a summary.

Revising Your Research Report

Once your first draft is finished, it is time to revise and proofread what you have written. Use this checklist to determine if you have met your goals of writing a clear, well-organized report.

- ☐ Is your thesis clearly stated?

- ☐ Do your report paragraphs follow in a clear, logical order?

- ☐ Does your report follow the outline you wrote for yourself?

- ☐ Have you cited all your sources?

- ☐ Have you made sure you have not plagiarized any material?

- ☐ Are your ideas clear to the reader?

- ☐ Have you used good paragraph bridges and word bridges between ideas?

- ☐ Do you have clear topic sentences for each paragraph?

- ☐ Have you eliminated any sentence fragments?

- ☐ Have you used the same verb tense throughout?

- ☐ Do your subjects and verbs agree?

- ☐ Have you used descriptive verbs and nouns?

- ☐ Does your writing flow from one idea to the next smoothly?

- ☐ Have you varied your sentences with some long and some short?

- ☐ Have you corrected any misspelled words?

- ☐ Have you corrected any errors in punctuation?

- ☐ Have you used active verbs rather than passive ones?

- ☐ Have you avoided using slang or jargon?

- ☐ Does your report avoid language that generalizes unfairly about people based on gender, ethnic group, religion, class, or age?

Citing Resources

The importance of accurately citing resources used when writing a research report cannot be overstated. It is absolutely necessary. The basic rules for citing resources are as follows:

- Always write the author's last name first, followed by a comma, then the first name. If there is more than one author of the work, write the first author's last name first, followed by a comma and the first name, then list the rest of the authors.

- Begin the first line of an entry on the left margin of the page, then indent ¹/₂ inch for the remaining lines of that entry.

- Double-space all entries.

- Capitalize the first letter of each word in titles.

- Underline (or italicize, if using a computer) the names of books, journals, magazines, newspapers, and films.

Basic Forms of Citations

A book

Epstein, Norrie. *The Friendly Shakespeare*. Viking Press, New York, 1993.

A part of a book (such as an essay or an article from a collection of articles)

Feynman, Richard P. "Atoms in Motion." *The World Treasury of Physics, Astronomy, and Mathematics*. Edited by Timothy Ferries. United States of America, 1991. Pages 3-17.

An article in a periodical (such as a newspaper or magazine)

Cox, Beverly and Martin Jacobs. "Spirit of the Harvest." *Native People Magazine*. Volume 10, Number 2 (1997): Pages 12–17.

A Web page

Nigro, Frank G. Franxfiles. Revised 18 January 1999. 21 June 1999.
http://shastacollege.edu/english/fnigro/.

Citing Resources *(cont.)*

An article in an online journal or magazine

Aschkenas, Lea. "Ivory Tower." *Salon Magazine*. January 1999.

> http://www.salonmagazine.com/it/

Book with no author named

Encyclopedia of Photography. New York: Crown, 1984.

An interview that you conducted

Rogers, Melvin R. Personal Interview. 12 November 1999.

An advertisement

Toyota. Advertisement. *San Jose Mercury-News*. 15 January 1999: 8–9.

Information from a CD-ROM

The CIA World Factbook. CD-ROM. Minneapolis: Quanta, 1992.

E-mail

Julius Orange. E-mail to the author. January 1999.

An article from a reference book

"Mandarin." *Encyclopedia Americana*. 1980.

A government publication

United States Department of Labor. Bureau of Statistics. *Dictionary of Occupational Titles*. 4th ed. Washington: GPO, 1977.

An online encyclopedia

"Fresco." *Britannica Online*. Verx. 97.1.1. March 1997. Encyclopedia Britannica. 29 March 1997.

> http://www.eb.com/180>

Using Footnotes and Endnotes

There are two places in your research report where you must cite your resources: in the body of the paper and at the end in the bibliography. There are three different forms that can be used when citing resources in the body of the report. The three forms are footnotes, endnotes, and parenthetical citations. The forms differ in how you cite your sources within the text of your essay. Your teacher may require that you use one form or another. **Ask your teacher which form to use.**

Using Footnotes

Footnotes are citations that appear at the end of each page within the text of the report itself. A number is placed in superscript at the end of the sentence, clause, or passage being cited[1] and at the beginning of the citation at the bottom of the page. Footnotes should be single-spaced with the first line indented. Place the name of the author of the work cited in normal order; do not place the last name first. Separate the author's name from the rest of the information with a comma and place the publication data within parentheses. There is no period at the end of the citation. If it is necessary to do so, you may carry part of the footnote to the next page.

The following is an example of how to write a footnote when the source is a magazine article or journal:

[1] Robert Upham, "GUH-JEE-GWAH-AL—LACROSS: A GIFT FROM THE CREATOR TO THE IROQUOIS AND THE WORLD," *Native People Magazine* (Phoenix, AZ, Spring, 1997), page 26. (Here you may write any comments you have concerning the materials being cited and continue it onto the next page if necessary.)

Using Endnotes

Endnotes are citations that appear at the end of the chapter, book, or research report. Endnotes are popular with many writers because they make an easier transition from text to citation than do footnotes. Footnotes can be intrusive for both the reader and the writer. Endnotes are marked within the report just as footnotes are. A number is placed in superscript at the end of the sentence, clause, or passage,[2] however, the source of the materials is placed at the end of the report rather than at the bottom of the page. The sources are listed in the order in which they appear in the report.

Use this form for the endnote.

[2] Robert Upham, "GUH-JEE-GWAH-AL—LACROSS: A GIFT FROM THE CREATOR TO THE IROQUOIS AND THE WORLD," *Native People Magazine* (Phoenix, AZ, Spring 1997) page 26. (Here you may write any comments you have concerning the material being cited.)

Using Parenthetical Citations

Parenthetical citations are the easiest to use when writing or reading. To make a parenthetical citation, simply place the name of the author and page number of the source in parentheses at the place where the source has been referred. The complete bibliographical information for the source is placed at the end of the report. The following paragraph is an example of a parenthetical citation within the body of a report and the bibliographical note which would appear at the end.

      The dashing Civil War hero appealed to the heart of the petite and pretty young woman as no one else could. When he was killed at the Battle of Little Bighorn, she wasted no time in establishing him as an even greater hero than he had portrayed himself in the press (Robbins 1).

The note at the end of the essay would be shown in the bibliography or works cited section as shown here:

Robbins, Mari Lu. "Elizabeth Bacon Custer: Myth Maker." *How to Write a Research Report*. Westminster, CA: Teacher Created Resources, Inc. 1999.

_____

Practice writing footnotes, endnotes, and parenthetical citations.
Write a phrase or sentence in which you will use information from one of your sources. Use a superscript as you would if you were using a footnote or endnote form of citation.

_____

_____

Write the citation for this source. _____

_____

Rewrite your phrase or sentence using a parenthetical citation. _____

_____

Write the citation for this source. _____

_____

Think about it and discuss it with your class.
How do the forms differ?
Which is easier to write?

Model Report

The following is a research report for you to use as a model as you write your own report. Examine the overall appearance of the report and citations. Also, see if you are able to identify the thesis statement and the word and paragraph transitions. What else do you note about the report?

Elizabeth Bacon Custer: Myth Maker

Elizabeth Bacon Custer's childhood and young adulthood prepared her for the life she was to fulfill: myth maker for her husband, George Armstrong Custer, whom she kept in the imagination of generations of Americans, as he had kept himself for years before that. She was born and raised an only child in the affluent home of a judge. After her mother died when she was 12, she learned to manipulate her way through life in the pleasant way allowed women in the Victorian Era,[1] filling her dreams with Victorian tales of romance and her mind with religion. The dashing Civil War hero appealed to the heart of the petite and pretty young woman as no one else could. When he was killed at the Battle of Little Bighorn, she wasted no time in establishing him as an even greater hero than he had portrayed himself in the press.[2]

When the young Libbie's mother died, her father, Judge Daniel Bacon, sent her to live with an aunt and two cousins, who indulged her every whim. She found that playing the role of the poor orphan child was her way to go. It got her much attention, all of it satisfying, for who would want to injure or hurt this pretty young thing who had lost so much already? When a few months later, Judge Bacon enrolled her in a private seminary for young ladies, she was well prepared to accept the special privileges given her by the principal, Mr. Erasmus Boyd. She became the only student in the school

---

[1] Shirley A. Leckie, *Elizabeth Bacon and the Making of a Myth* (Norman: Univ. of Okalahoma Press, 1993) page 12

[2] Lawrence A. Frost, *The Custer Album.* (Seattle, WA: Superior Publishing Co., 1964) page 178

Model Report *(cont.)*

to have not only a room shared with her favorite teacher, but also a private parlor with a view of Lake Erie and a garden all her own in which to raise the flowers she loved.

Libbie also loved to read. Her favorite authors were Fanny Fern and Grace Greenwood.[3] These writers were very influential on the young girl's mindset, with their often flowery, romantic themes. One of Greenwood's poems, "A Morning Ride," begins this way and spoke to Libbie's heart:

> "When troubled in spirit, when weary of life
> When I faint 'neath its burdens, and shrink from its strife,
> When its fairest scene seems but a desolate waste;
> Then come ye not near me my sad heart to cheer
> With friendship's soft accents, or sympathy's tear;
> No counsel I ask, and no pity I need,
> But bring me, oh, bring me, my gallant young steed!
> With his high arch'd neck and his nostril spread wide,
> His eye full of fire, and his step full of pride!
> As I spring to his back, as I seize the strong rein,
> The strength of my spirit returneth again!"[4]

The books and poetry Libbie read filled her mind with thoughts of a handsome, romantic young husband. Women were not allowed in the professions or most jobs at the time.

Many young men came to call on Libbie, for she was charming, petite, and talented. Then one night she dreamed she had married a soldier in the army. In her dream, she hid from rebels with her love and was forced to kill someone in self-defense. Her dream "ended beautifully."[5] Not long after that dream, when a dashing young army officer on leave from the Civil War came calling, she was ready to fall in love.

---

[3] Leckie, ibid. page 12

[4] Grace Greenwood, University of Michigan, February 1999
http://www.hti.umich.edu/bin/amv-idx.pl?type=HTML&rgn- DIVO&byte=15182606

[5] Leckie, ibid. page 22

Model Report *(cont.)*

They married. She was twenty-two, and he was twenty-five, the golden-haired fearless, dare-devil hero of the Civil War. But only twelve years later, Custer was dead on a hillside in Montana. Libbie devoted the rest of her life to making sure the memory of her husband would be forever that of a hero.

The stories she actively encouraged included one of Custer making a gallant last stand at the Battle of Little Bighorn as hordes of howling Indians surrounded him. He was so portrayed in Buffalo Bill's Wild West Show and movies starring the biggest stars of their time. What has since been claimed by Native Americans, historians, and archaeologists is that rather than being a brave hero, Custer was a rash glory-hunter who placed his troops in jeopardy. Had he obeyed orders, the tragedy would have been prevented. As long as she lived, Libbie Custer gave speeches, dedicated memorial statues to her husband, and wrote books praising his courage and kindness, nurturing what has since been called the "Custer Myth." Custer remains, in the hearts of many, high on a hill with glory all around him, for Libbie outlived those who would have told the truth about her husband. She got the last word as long as she lived.

Bibliography

Frost, Lawrence. A. *The Custer Album.* Seattle WA: Superior Publishing Company, 1964.

Greenwood, Grace. "A Morning Ride." University of Michigan. February 1999.
http://www.hti.umich.edu/bin/amv-idx.pl?type=HTML&rgn.DIVO&byte=15182606

Leckie, Shirley A. *Elizabeth Bacon Custer and the Making of a Myth.* Norman, OK: University of Oklahoma Press, 1993.

Smiley, Robin H. "The Battle of the Little Bighorn in Fiction." *First the Book Collector's Magazine.* May 1998: pages 24–35.

Glossary of Research Terms

Abstract—Summary of an article in a journal, usually found at the beginning of the article.

Almanac—Reference put out each year with selected facts, such as weather and statistical information.

Alphabetical—Listing in order of the alphabet.

APA—American Psychological Association

Autobiography—The story of a person's life as told by that person.

Bibliography—List of books, journal and periodical articles, CD-ROMs, and Internet sites at the end of a book or journal article. Leads to additional information.

Biography—The story of a person's life as told by another person.

Book Stacks—Shelves where reference and circulating books are located.

Call Number—The group of letters and numbers given to a book in a library. Shows the order in which one book is arranged with other books on the shelves.

Citation—Written information about source materials such as books, periodicals, and journals used in an article. Identifies author, page numbers, volume number, publisher, and publishing date.

Dictionary—A book listing words alphabetically with their pronunciations and meanings. There are general dictionaries, as well as specialized subject dictionaries.

Document—Show evidence.

Encyclopedia—Reference book which provides facts and background information.

Journal—Magazine published by a group or institution, usually concentrated on a specific subject area and written by educators or researchers. Magazines found in newsstands are not generally journals.

Journal Index—Alphabetical listing of journal articles. It may be a general index or may be specific to a field such as medicine, technology, or education.

MLA—Modern Language Association

Source—Any book, magazine, newspaper, TV show, person, or Web site used in a report or article.

Resources

Ackermann, Ernest. *Learning to Use the Internet—An Introduction with Examples and Exercises.* Franklin, Beedl & Associates, 1995.

Baron, Alvin Ph. D. *Bud's Easy Research Paper Computer Manual,* Second Edition. Lawrence House Publishers, Lawrence, New York, 1998.

Butler, Mark. *How to Use the Internet.* Ziff-Davis Press, 1994.

Fowler, Allan. *The Library of Congress.* Children's Press, 1996.

Gardner, Paul. *Internet for Teachers and Parents.* Teacher Created Resources, 1996.

Giagnocavo, Gregory, Tim McLain, and Vince Distefano. *Educator's Internet Companion.* Wentworth Worldwide Media, Inc., 1995.

Haag, Tim. *Internet for Kids.* Teacher Created Resources, 1996.

Hardendorff, Jeanne B. *Libraries and How to Use Them.* Franklin Watts, 1979.

McLain, Tim and Vince Distefano. *Educator's Worldwide Web Tour Guide.* Wentworth Worldwide Media, Inc., 1995.

Null, Kathleen Christopher. *How to Give a Presentation.* Teacher Created Resources, 1998.

Pederson, Ted & Francis Moss. *Internet for Kids! A Beginner's Guide to Surfing the Net.* Price Stern Sloan, Inc., 1995.

Periera, Linda. *Computers Don't Byte.* Teacher Created Resources, 1996.

Salzman, Marian & Robert Pondiscio. *The Ultimate On-Line Homework Helper.* Avon Books, 1996.

Internet Sites

Farmer's Almanac.com: http://www.almanac.com/
all sorts of information including weather, puzzles, and facts

Best Information on the Net: http://www.sau.edu/bestinfo.html
databases, general reference, news, picture sources, Internet resources, electronic reading room

The World Fact Book: http://www.odci.gov/cia/publications/factbook/country-frame.html
countries, reference maps, facts about every country—climate, boundaries, terrain, etc.

My Virtual Reference Desk: http://www.refdesk.com/index.html?search=steinway&list=index.html
everything from acronyms to USA and world newspapers

Step by Step—Research & Writing IPL: http://www.ipl.org/teen/aplus/step1.htm

Research-It!—Your One-Stop Reference Desk: http://www.itools.com/research-it/research-it.html

Electronic Reference Desk: http://scholes.alfred.edu/Ref.html

The Great American Website: http://www.uncle-sam.com/

Common Types of Papers: http://www.ipl.org/teen/aplus/linkscommon.htm

The Writer's Handbook: http://www.wisc.edu/writing/Handbook/PlanResearchPaper.html

The Research Paper: http://www.chesapeake.edu/Writingcenter/respaper.html

The Columbia Guide to Online Style: http://www.columbia.edu/cu/cup/cgos/idxbasic.html

Purdue University Online Writing Lab: http://owl.english.purdue.edu/html

Writing Center Page Chesapeake College: http://www.chesapeake.edu/Writingcenter/respaper.html

Basic Guide to Essay Writing: http://members.tripod.com/-lklivingston/essay/

Writer's Handbook University of Wisconsin: http://www.wisc.edu/writing/Handbook/PlanResearchPaper.html

Answer Key

Dewey Decimal System, page 11

1. 880; 2. 390; 3. 270; 4. 430; 5. 930; 6. 620; 7. 790; 8. 070; 9. 180; 10. 540; 11. 270; 12. 300; 13. 980; 14. 750; 15. 820; 16. 910; 17. 410; 18. 760; 19. 090; 20. 570.

Fact and Opinion, page 14 (Accept appropriate answers.)

1. Opinion—Some people do not like dogs, some are allergic to dogs, etc.

2. Fact

3. Opinion—Although knowing another language is desirable, it is possible to live a full life without it.

4. Fact

5. Opinion—Some students need to study more, some less.

6. Fact

7. Opinion—Some people are allergic to milk.

8. Opinion—Some parents do, and some parents do not.

9. Opinion—Some people like this movie, and some do not.

10. Fact

11. Opinion—Some people like *Time* magazine and some do not.

12. Fact

13. Fact—Tabloid magazines and papers, for example, often print stories which verge on fantasy.

14. Opinion—The facts in an almanac will be interesting to some people and not to others. .

Quiz on Critical Thinking, page 16

1. C—Your neighbor may or may not have good information, and what he has is probably biased. Dr. Dean Edell, while very knowledgeable, may not have studied this question lately. *The Physician's Desk Reference of Drugs and Alcohol Abuse* will have recent and accurate information on the subject.

2. B—An article in *Newsweek*, while probably not the best source of all, will be more accurate on this subject than *MAD*, which is not a news magazine, or a political program, which is probably pushing a certain political viewpoint.

3. C—Bell's invention of the telephone.

4. A—The technology person in your school will probably be more aware of the best current materials and equipment for schools than will the owner of a store or a software company president who wants to sell something.

5. A—In this case, you probably want to ask your family doctor, because he/she is the one who has "been in the field" in a personal way and can give you some sound advice about what being a doctor is like.

6. C—*The Bulletin of the Center for Disease Control* has data from all over the country. Your school health aide knows only what is happening in your school, and your teacher probably knows only what is happening in his/her classroom.

Online Research Quiz page 18

1. YES 2. YES 3. NO 4. YES 5. YES 6. YES 7. YES 8. YES 9. YES 10. NO 11. NO 12. NO 13. YES 14. YES 15. NO 16. YES 17. YES 18. YES